TALKING TO THE WIND

ALSO BY RICHARD WEHRMAN

The Book of the Garden

Light was Everywhere: Poems by Richard Wehrman

Dialogues with Death

TALKING
TO
THE
WIND

RICHARD WEHRMAN

Merlinwood Books · East Bloomfield, NY

Copyright © 2016 by Richard Wehrman

All Rights Reserved
Printed in the United States of America
First Edition
ISBN: 978-0-9913882-4-0

Merlinwood Books
P.O. Box 146
E. Bloomfield NY 14443

www.richardwehrman.com

For
Paul, Dale, and Tomek

CONTENTS

I

ALL ON ITS OWN   *1*
WE WERE GIVEN   *2*
THE HOPE OF THE WORLD   *3*
WARDROBE   *4*
OVER AND OVER   *5*
FUEL AND FIRE   *7*
DESCENT   *8*
ANGEL   *9*
ADVENT   *10*
THIS WE DO WITH THE LIVING   *11*
THE ONE WE SOUGHT   *12*
CRYSTAL LETTERS   *13*
REVERBERATION   *14*
THE NINETY-NINE NAMES   *15*
CONSUMED BY BEAUTY   *16*
SHAKEN   *17*
FLINT AND TINDER   *18*
COMPLETION   *19*
LODESTONE   *20*
THE ALLOWED   *21*
POTENTIA   *22*
IN A DIFFERENT WAY   *23*
NO WAY TO STAY BY HOLDING   *24*
WHAT DID YOU SAY?   *25*
UP CLOSE   *26*
WHERE WE LIVED   *27*

OUT OF IRON *28*

COLD OCTOBER *29*

A QUESTION *30*

REMEMBERING *31*

GO NOW *32*

RETURN *33*

II

THE GARDENER *37*

ONE TURN *38*

THE GOLDEN DOORWAY *39*

RUBBER BOOTS *40*

O WIND *41*

I WILL LOVE YOU *42*

INSIDE OUT *43*

BLOW! BLOW! *44*

WHAT WE LIVED THROUGH *45*

IT WAS THEN *46*

WAKING *47*

CLEANING THE DRIVEWAY IN SPRING *48*

CRAZY MIND *49*

III

I WAS NEVER WRONG *53*

SIX SHORT POEMS *54*

MORNING LIGHT, CLOUDS, WIND *55*

THE DAY BEGINS *56*

FOREVERNESS *57*

FULL OUT *58*

FOR YOU *59*

THE MARCH *60*

AFTERNOON, JULY *61*
LAUGHING AT ACCOMPLISHMENT *62*
RELAX *63*
TO A LOST LAPIS *64*
THE WORLD WAS THERE *65*
POURING *66*
MORNING *67*
TUTOR *68*
EVENING RAIN *69*
OUT OF EARTH *70*
VIBRATION *71*
VIOLET *72*

IV

EACH STAR PLACED IN THE NIGHT SKY *75*
LIKE A RIVER, LIKE AN OCEAN *76*
WE CAME TOGETHER *77*
THE WAY THERE *78*
DRAINING AWAY *79*
IT'S LIKE NOTHING *80*
GIVING *81*
LIKE WATER *82*
ONE STEP *83*
SAYING NOTHING *84*
HOW IT IS *85*
BODHISATTVA *86*
EVENING COMING ON *87*
MORE THAN ENOUGH *88*
ONLY THE BUDDHA *89*
LOST IN MYSELF *90*
EVERYTHING WAS THERE *91*

UPON THE WALL *92*

THE POSSIBILTY OF RULES *93*

UNHOLDABLE *94*

WHEN IT IS *95*

V

OLD CROWS *99*

BETWEEN OUR FINGERTIPS *100*

THE SOLID WEIGHT OF BEING *101*

KATHY *102*

BRILLIANCE TOO BRIGHT *103*

TURNING COLDER *104*

IT IS TIME *105*

TASTED BY BEAUTY *106*

A DIFFERENT KIND OF HOLY *107*

ENOUGH *108*

MORNING LIGHT *109*

THE SNOW *110*

SATURDAY MORNING, 8:00 A.M. *111*

IN OUR BONES *112*

WHEN I FELL INTO THE WORLD *113*

TALKING TO THE WIND

I

ALL ON ITS OWN

Blank paper, empty pen.
What will leak out—the whole
world, or a single tiny flower?
Here, it's already started!
Whatever wants to be, coming into
being, all on its own.

WE WERE GIVEN

And the Light
broke wide upon the Earth,
and we were given,
again, the point of
turning, the
step of our own foot, forward;
the choice, to
bear the better year,
to not turn back,
to lift the weight we wished
for ages was not
ours to bear,
to lift the beauty of the orbits
onward, swinging into
springs of who-knows-what,
emboldened by a chance,
a crack in emptiness
to give it all, to
stand by Her who births
us out again,
into a virgin year, wherein
by dying absolutely to the old—
that was so dead already—
comes forth
what we do not deserve,
but are the only vessels
able to receive,
The New.

THE HOPE OF THE WORLD

We are the gift
we have searched for,
over rocks and streams,
through deserts and
knife-edged plains—

we were seeds searching for earth,
for the warm dark humus to hold us,
not knowing—but absolutely knowing—
that *she* would bring us forth,

though it took a hundred years,
one day our rough branches would blossom,
bearing this golden fruit,

and we would turn and see—
we stand within
an Orchard.

WARDROBE

Set upon the floor, a worn valise;
within, the threadbare clothes,
the curled old leather shoes.

So do I put these on again,
and stain the pristine body?

Do I wear again the
ancient self of suffering,
or clothe myself
in stars?

OVER AND OVER

Brainless wonder,
man without a mind—
who do you think is here,
looking out of your eyes,
reading these words?

Without a history,
without your old story,
who sits here in this
broken-down body,
brand new?

You carry around
yesterday's accomplishments
in your worn leather satchel,
thinking *who you were* has
something to do with
who you are.
If you were mistaken then,
what about now?

Rabbits and deer leave
piles of little round pellets;
even a snail leaves a trail of slime.
Why keep stirring your
own excrement, looking
for answers?

Let your own being blossom
outside of who you think you
are—let the bud break through
this husk of thinking
you are someone,

and let this
marvelous Awareness
taste the sweetness
that flows out from the place
you used to call
your own
individual soul.

FUEL AND FIRE

Did you think
God was not stronger
than your depression,
that the difficulties
that defeat you
could somehow defeat God?
Remember,
the maker creates
what he will,
and the drag of his arm
sweeps all of it
away.
Your despair
gives no credit
to the One who made you,
who placed love
within your heart,
where you now
feel only ash.
Feed upon the fuel
of divine creativity
and blow unceasingly
until the spark
catches flame.
Remember, *He* is far stronger
than your depression,
and continually gives you
new breath
with which to
blow.

DESCENT

Like the slow
tick of the clock,
the unnoticed moment passed,
where you crossed a divide,
not knowing you had,
and were set down on another side,
one that you mistook for ascent,
when in fact you were descending,
where you never intended
to go, imagining a world
where things only rose,
rather than fell.

ANGEL

O angel of myself, inform me.
Let flow from your celestial sphere
the radiant presence of Yourself,
let it, in me, overflow this one who never knew,
who tried, and failed, and tried again,
who ached for you in ignorance of You who ached for me.
Fill me, O Radiant Self, with our bright destiny.
Let my incompleteness vanish with your rising Being,
let your transcendent Truth, through me
be present in the World.

ADVENT

The gift
came from the sensed,
the unseen;
it sought out the dark,
falling forward
into tomorrow,
being birthed backward,
from that time,
not yet here when we
retired, when we
fell away into the calling
arms of dreams—
now this low wind roaring
and the light flooding
our bodies as the curtains
are drawn back,
to white snow
and new earth
everywhere.

THIS WE DO WITH THE LIVING

Folded blanket on the bed,
curtains opened
to the sky;
the darkness lifts in inches
with our steadiness
of breath—
this we do with every living thing:
abide in patience,
witness to our fears
and in our certain knowledge,
the moments one by one
that bring the dawn.

THE ONE WE SOUGHT

It takes
a day or a week
for it to pour out,
what we spent
so much time holding away,
by the rushing around,
the endless errands
when quiet was calling—
a curled leaf,
the twisted wire of the
headphones, the
small colored stones
that sit so still
staring back at you,
casting their
shadow,
brilliant in the white
artificial light
that cannot hide,
no matter how brightly,
the tiny folds of wrinkled
skin, wrapped around
the one we sought,
the one who
was here,
all along.

CRYSTAL LETTERS

Pale sky,
barest blue-grey
milk-light,
gives of itself
interweaving
snowflakes falling;
numberless crystal letters
from *you*, in no
way diminishing
emptiness forever,
falling into
form.

REVERBERATION

Wind in the morning—today
there is no wind.
Only the darkness of early rising,
refreshed and wide awake.

Thin snow greets the grate
the snowplow makes on its run,
roaring up the road
and back again.

What seemed like another day
is a new day—
old sounds struck new
on this worn bronze bell.

THE NINETY-NINE NAMES

Marvelous,
vision's gift,
the sight of our eyes.

Captured by beauty,
falling within
each form.

What wonder!
At sunrise, at snowfall,
at flowers in spring.

With breath
and with being,
wherever we look,
you, seen everywhere.

CONSUMED BY BEAUTY

I gazed on beauty,
on my great desire,
my hands and face pressed flat
against the window glass,
and ached for consummation to possess
the One whose beauty
far outshone the rest.

Then I was changed.
The glass dissolved,
and I was moving inward losing
all my edges—
and discovered as
I thinned away from view,

I was no longer *me*,
but was consumed by beauty
into *You*.

SHAKEN

What can I say
when the ground
gives way,
when solid turns liquid,
when the steady beat
turns ragged?
Why are we amazed
that the solid
is shaken,
we who grip these bodies
with talons of iron,
as though we never knew
our backs bore wings, that
our journey is made
of light, that
our ability is to pass through,
to be made
of anything
at all.

FLINT AND TINDER

Where is
the movement of desire,
the heat to have,
the pull of beaten wings to flame?

For all seems cold,
an ash that settles like the snow.

I am in need of kindling:
a spark struck home from stone
into these arid tindered tissue folds;

yet I am damp and soaked
from winter's frozen rain,
and seem incapable
of burning.

COMPLETION

Placed upon the earth,
we offered ourselves to
whatever would come.
We were stones
worn away,
in the grinding of rivers,
in the breath of the air.
Where we willed, we were wrong.
Where we opened,
we were lifted and carried.
We tried to choose:
we learned instead to be chosen.
We struggled to endure—
maybe for all the wrong reasons—
but we did,
right to the end,
and this was our strength.
This was what
you said it would take—
and we gave,
as you asked—
everything.

—for William Vasel, (1939—2011)

LODESTONE

Feet like iron,
pulled to the center of the earth,
the gravity mass,
choir of dense angels,
singing of attraction.

THE ALLOWED

In patience,
in unimposing presence,
in mutual searching,
in truth's abiding,
in non-judgment;
in open questioning,
in heart's receiving,
in widening understanding,
there heart arises,
as sun rises,
warming and brightening:
now peacefulness,
now love.

POTENTIA

The difference
had arrived here
before me,
a certain sense of a
phantom limb,
the lifting an absence,
what wasn't here,
but invisible,
as it was in its presence,
so how would you know,
but you knew,
and that was
its way back in,
like the scratch of a wire,
metallic in irritation,
but a memory,
at least in the moment,
for all was quiet,
like the center
of a stone,
waiting in the dark
for light.

IN A DIFFERENT WAY

Let the day
arrive in a different way,
let my greeting be of strangers
bearing gifts, welcomed without fear,
falling into wonder as each moment opens,
bearing the next new thing,
a doorway opening outward,
into deeper depths,
into greater Light.

NO WAY TO STAY BY HOLDING

The curse,
caught in the vine,
the twisted turn of the ropes,
the bind of the past,
the way it was,
the way it should work, but no
longer does;
the seeing of that,
the knowing of how it is gone,
is going,
is fading in front of us, yes,
yet the ropes pull,
the constriction binds,
and it burns,
as though we must lose our actual skin,
impossibly leave what we are, die—
not as a word but an actuality—
give up our very selves,
that are that past,
that dissolved in substantiality, and
do what we cannot do,
slip from the shell defenseless,
into what we can't possibly stand,
but were born to,
leaping out of the past
into the now.

WHAT DID YOU SAY?

It was *thou shalt not*
and *you should*,

It was *what did you say?*
and *don't use that tone of voice*

with me young man.
It was *your guilt* and *your shame*,

every way you learned that
you were bad, not good enough,

a failure in the eyes of
those you loved,

or thought you did, until
they said those words

that turned you inside out—
not knowing that you did—

telling all the world for so long after,
how much that they loved you,

how happy was the childhood
that you lived.

UP CLOSE

All of a sudden
it is all up close,
not you back there
and the world out here,
but like when
we were six or seven,
before fear reached out at us;
back when the world
was made of real things:
brick and grass,
peaches and sharp gravel,
the way it is today,
now that despair
and this cynical knowledge
has dried up,
turned to dust, and
blown away.

WHERE WE LIVED

Dear house, old home, you have moved into
another realm, passed into a new history, not of our own.
You still open your rooms, your walls, to my soul.
There you are ageless, container for growth,
bright and evil chrysalis of my life.
Basement to attic you acted, agent upon me.
Your yard the first garden of Eden, your stones
and gravel the Roman road to hell.
Old specter, old shelter, live on until our need dissolves.
Holder and incubator, vessel of Vesta,
your role was precious. For your faults be forgiven.
For your gifts, be forever blessed.

—Upon the sale of our childhood home in St. Louis, Missouri.

OUT OF IRON

How many times
does iron enter the fire?
How often does boiling
free us to air, to our continual
re-condensation?
Over and again,
the heating, the beating,
the plunge and the gasp.
We think we know
the maker's intention, who
thrusts us to the brink
and pulls us back.
But all we know is the heat
of his furnace, his anvil.
The hammer swings
and we receive:
bright strength,
keen edge of sharpness,
Beauty held ascendant.

COLD OCTOBER

Cold October nights
and I dream of separations;
the *Day of the Dead* approaches,
and I walk in my old ways,
unaware. Yet something grabs my
cold bones, pointing me toward
the mirror—*this was why
you traveled North, remember?*
My old master now travels
the invisible realm; old
friends and long-lost lovers—
all like bent trees and
bare branches, blown in the wind.
This love of life points
me back toward the *bardos*, to
preparing for a long journey—
one with no money or suitcase,
only the longings
of the Heart.

A QUESTION

Did you carry the gift?
Or did you set it down,
intending to return,
forgetting your reason,

while bringing water to your lips,
as you raised the tent roof,
as your child called your name,
as your wisdom and stature grew,
as your wife and friends turned old?

Did you carry the gift and
and give it freely?

Or did you wander away,
to lock the door in the night,
with no fault and no guilt,
and simply
forget?

REMEMBERING

Old body, be not afraid,
though fear is what you do so well.
    We began this journey brand new—
you, all combinations of cosmos,
me, newly returned from
a journey past the stars.
    Together we've wandered all over
this great earth, trying to remember
who we were.
    Memory returned slowly—
a fragment of melody, a sunrise
on a winter day, in the birth
of a new year.
    One day we'll say goodbye
and travel our separate ways, returning
to the wholeness of everything.
    On that day we'll remember
each other precisely. And astonishment,
not fear, will be the last thing
on our mind.

GO NOW

There are some who say,
if we're going,
let's go now;
we'll pack a lunch,
row out to the edge,
and wait.

And I say, I'll stay.
I'll wait with the raindrops
from last night's storm. I'll wait
for the sun's heat and the next hard
rain that comes.

However long that
might take.

    —(Upon reading Anne Sexton's *The Awful Rowing Toward God*)

RETURN

Do you remember
how we all climbed aboard,
how we hugged and held each other
as the ship moved deeper, out into the stars?
How we promised we'd remember,
how we said *"somehow I'll find you"*
And then as we leapt
one after another into that starlit emptiness,
aiming with our disappearing wings,
for the blue ball with
the white moon?
Remember how fast we fell?
How the wind whipped our faces and
blew each memory away?
How we found ourselves
in the warm darkness, tiny and growing,
each breathing our whole selves breathlessly,
with each beat of our heart.

II

THE GARDENER

The year has
turned, and Spring
is months away,
but a new thing,
bright,
like the smallest seed
has arrived,
fertile and filled
with promise,
with mystery,
with miracles.
And my water will be Trust,
And my soil will
be my Soul,
and its food will
be No Fear,
and I will be—
bright *I* will be,
the Gardener.

ONE TURN

Some days
we think direction
does not matter;
wall or window,
one is as good as another.
So simple is the turning;
a child's spinning
becomes the old man,
set in his one way.
Here you are,
staring into your
black cave of sorrows;
while with
one turn towards the light,
warmth is upon you,
and shadows—
into which you long
stared and
pondered—
have vanished
and returned as
joy.

THE GOLDEN DOORWAY

The pencil comes to the page—
and nothing comes.

There should be something
—but nothing comes.

And I remember the gift,
how everything flows into being
and out again—

This is a blessing, not a curse.

This is the doorway in
to beginning,
this *nothing*.

RUBBER BOOTS

Winter has ground me down again;
snow and ice heaves the broken world,
piles of dirty ice leave the detritus
of centuries.

But look! It's spring again!
Birds sing like there's no tomorrow.
Worms blink their eyes and pop
out of the soil.

An old man like me gets grumpy
on these cold wet grey days.

But inside a young boy grins,
eager to stomp rubber boots in puddles,
to send water flying
everywhere!

O WIND

Wind-roaring howling wind,
cornstalk wheat-dragging tree-throwing wind,
avalanche-falling Niagara-thundering wind,
planet-tilting continent-sliding
gravity-sucking wind,
bodies forced flat, ears flared back, hair-streaming,
arms covering

O Wind! O fierce wind!

mover of land mass,
particle thrower, bird blower, pass by, pass over,
blow away, blow out,
blow on.

I WILL LOVE YOU

The slow snow went, wet, back in,
received by the green grass, open-armed
in a deep drink, a loving sink,
saying—*welcome home wet one,
such a cold shoulder*, but I—
I will make you warm, I will love you
until you sweat like tears.

INSIDE OUT

It's almost there,
beginning to burst,
right at the outer edge,
the pieces you can't see
if you don't look,
and looking,
there they are,
not a haze but a hint,
mostly stick and twig and bark,
ground by winter's grit,
ice and snow-whipped wind—
but now a tenderness,
a turning inside out,
pale green for our pink,
swelling, reaching for air,
for light,
breaking past protection,
opening up,
breathing all inside
out.

BLOW! BLOW!

Blow in the wind
blows free and throws
the willow into river,
the lilac buds have burst
and tiny leaves have
dropped their fists declaring:
we wait upon no other!
Winter's dead, cold winds
and snows no matter—our time's
our own and we were
coming all the while you filled your
head with rusted dreams, despairs
and frozen axles.
The wheel turns eternal
whether what you will,
so climb aboard and feel
the wind blow free;
your mind's been freed by
all this sudden air, and
something bright has
overturned your soul.

WHAT WE LIVED THROUGH

I would
feel your flower,
your inwardness
drawn out,
the haze,
the breath about,
purity grown green,
too poor a word
for inside
reaching out,
a light grown
form like
feathers, river fingers
wound, the lift
of air surround
the rigid stem
of what we
have lived through—
and since we lived,
gave forth,
with our whole
heart, anew.

IT WAS THEN

You come in,
the most particular
of God,
recognized in the
beginning
by your indivisible
glow.
It was then
my heart opened
and flowed into you—
and You, in your Beauty,
held me in your
arms, and flowed
unceasingly
into Me.

WAKING

Sunlight shocked
the new-leaved locust,
the darkened room
around;

my eyes but
half awake,
as yellow-gold and green
poured down—

bloomed from within a dream,
reality shone bright;

I stumbled into mystery,
into color,
form, and
Light.

CLEANING THE DRIVEWAY IN SPRING

Master of the house—
do you feel betrayed?
Did you think our
agreement was one
of eternity?
That I would lie here forever,
smooth and unchanged,
baking in summer sun,
freezing in winter ice—
that my cracks would never show?
Am I better than you,
that fire and ice
would not break me apart,
as age has eroded
your youth?
Now I am returning to
my old ways—gravel, sand, and mud,
and the relief of returning
to formlessness.
May you be blessed
as well to fall apart completely,
to be released
from holding together
every single thing.

CRAZY MIND

Old Man Crazy Mind
               drives me crazy,
               won't let go
               I won't
comes to a cross road
               any road at all

"when you come to a fork in the road take it"

wanders on all day
               up over boulders
               down winding streams
maybe a rainbow from all those words
               cascading
               over the falls
riding unconcerned
               feet out front
               or over his head

Old Man Crazy Mind
               not caring
               going wherever
               this road takes him
try to follow
   no way no way
               letting all of it

go – *o* – *o* – *o* - *o*

III

I WAS NEVER WRONG

I was never wrong about the birdsong,

I was never wrong
about the grey weathered boards.

I was never wrong about cattails,
or the trees reflected along the river's bank.

Every autumn leaf or
roadside springtime flower
was my witness:

I held that hickory nut
and let it be astounding on its own.

The hovering moon,
the heron gliding down the mirror of the pond—
they rose as I rose, in that single instant.

Were we born, or did we die?
Were we right or wrong?

Close this book upon your lap and listen:
our cry will be the first sound
that you hear!

SIX SHORT POEMS

That low roar
of wind
in the cedars.

·

Last year's wisteria,
tangled in the
pine.

·

Curling brown vine, riding
up and down
in the wind.

·

Here, with myself,
at last.

·

Across the stubbled fields,
light breaks underneath
the gray clouds.

·

Caught, in the middle
of the day, I give
you, *this*.

MORNING LIGHT, CLOUDS, WIND

The window's light
upon the wall

    was coming, going,
    moving into blooming being,

expanding, shrinking,
all of it soft edges—

    branches waving, intersecting
    light-washed softness

here—within a heartbeat—gone

    a rise and fall and fade again,
    upon the wall and door

that seem content to to stay,
but past the presence

    of their staying, they too
    fade away.

THE DAY BEGINS

Morning. The quiet
circles around me, a huge
bowl of silence. Everything emerges—
a car rolling down the road, someone
knocking dishes in the sink.

My pencil makes a little scraping noise,
rough lead scratching over
thin paper pages.

All these movements sink
back into silence.

Quiet spreads out over miles of stubbled fields,
past bare trees and dark old barns.
Deer hold in their tracks,
fox and crows stand motionless,
watching.

The sounds of geese travel down the sky,
moving past the trees in a ragged line.
The back door slams and the
day begins,

one sound after another,
falling slowly out of silence and back
into time.

FOREVERNESS

Is it the foreverness,
the way summer days go on unending,
the empty blue skies,
the infinities of fresh air?
Or the way the day-lilies, already gone,
open their orange blossoms
morning after morning?
Or the eternity, past by mid-July,
of blackberries ripe and pierced by thorn?
Or the glowing morning glory,
gathering in the night to another day's unfurling,
with violet like no other, a preciousness
eternal, gone as we all are gathered,
by the end of the day.

FULL OUT

It's what they do—
run and wheel full out, tossing their manes,
released from their night stables
into the sunlit field.

Beyond the milkweed and
the Queen Anne's lace,
their hoof-beats hammer a field away,

their joy and strength fully-formed perfection,
launching the bright morning
into the cool and quiet air.

FOR YOU

The forehead-tensioned edge,
the tap of finger rippled
wells of widening rings, bells of touch
on a silent Saturday eve;
the slanting sun, the breath of air
relaxed, withheld, the willow leaves
bare movement in that ocean's ebb
and flow; and all about, in humid
yellow light, the cricket's high-pitched
whine and birdsong's distant watered
voice, all find their way across, above,
below, and through—the sound, the
sight, the fuel, all summer through and
through, with nowhere left for me
to be but inside every single thing;
the barn's been burned, the ancient
shed torn down, and *all flows into
being with such ease*, as though
all summer traveled sixteen billion miles
with nothing else to do, but *be* and
be and *be*, another billion miles,
for you.

THE MARCH

How can I keep from smiling,
as the fuzzy caterpillar
does his circus act,
balancing on the single angled cord
that holds the tent erect;
where halfway down he pauses,
swings his beaded head from side to side,
to see the world around him or
spy a leafy tree—then seeming
unconcerned, as though
it was the easiest thing to do,
continues down this rope between
two worlds, on his multiple feet that follow
one another, into the grass and
off towards dinner.

AFTERNOON, JULY

So like swimming,
this sinking down,
lower and deeper into the earth,
not mere dirt and rock
but leaf and warm air, beetle
and berry, lit by birds
and cantaloupe flowers,
thick, as the day stretches,
afternoon toward evening,
where those who work
drag home against its current—
while I, preceding them
lean back, floating on thick air,
in aromas of dry oats and
sun-hot wheat, buoyed by
the rush of resinous leaves,
loving the density
of a sweet summer day,
like a river winding its way,
undammed and unleveed,
stretching over hills and down
fields flowing, through
cherry and apple and
grape run wild,
flowing where it wants
to flow.

LAUGHING AT ACCOMPLISHMENT

Can anything arrive at the wrong time?
Do all actions, all understandings occur at
any other time than now, at this most perfect and
present of moments? Does not the heat, the snow,
the ice arrive in perfection; do our chills
and sweats, our beautiful fitful days
hold one drop more or less than what they are?
The truth of this moment laughs at accomplishment,
at getting somewhere. Haven't we always
been right here all along?

RELAX

Old Bankei certainly
knew that of which
he spoke.

Possessing neither Japanese
or English, he uses my mother's tongue,
reminding me to relax

every time the wind blows,
every time the cock crows.

TO A LOST LAPIS

Dear lapis, my rolling stone, my cosmos
creator, intimate echo of the night sky;
you who brought me the galaxy within,
the loving infinity of the star-strewn
night; be safe on your own night journey,
traveling on your own, seeking your own
lights. Bring your blessings to unknown
beings, astonish them as you did me,
fill their hearts with the safety of
our billion-year sky, the blanket of
bright ones watching, tending their sparkling
fires, looking down on us all, through
the dark night.

THE WORLD WAS THERE

Recovering our selves
we lost our selves,
the Silence more silent than water,
the light more liquid
than bird song,
the breath of the whole air
rolling like a slow wave;
we swam, we soared,
we did not move an inch,
the world was there where
we had been before;
blown we were, a dandelion globe
expanded to the stars,
where we float back to fall
within the great green
arms of God.

POURING

Something has happened,
this small tear in my side,
even the light spills out from
the lamp,
even the silence floods the room
to the window, to the roof—
warm holding is flowing,
is filling,
is coming from everything,
chair, cushion, pencil,
and shoe, my foot
warm inside it, rising in me
as the room, as we meet,
as we pour out into
each other

MORNING

Morning's sure hand
reached for me,
and raised me up
from night's long shadows,
and set before me
all that is, pristine,
washed with every color,
sound and smell
that earth possesses—
wherein I knew no lack,
and felt myself
at home among
all things and men.

TUTOR

Tutor in love,
teach me!
Bright eyes are smiling
from this gray day,
grandfather clock
swings a syncopated beat,
wind does his invisible dance
to and fro.
This spirit being inside me
claps his hands, calling out
See! Joy is real!
Today, working or sleeping
we are filled with dancing,
and loving everything
and everyone
we meet!

EVENING RAIN

The sky lowers, darkness gathers as
substance, the air is hushed, sound is withdrawn,
and before I can begin to write
the drops come; wide and openly spaced, spattering,
hesitant but sure of themselves, gathering lakes and rivers
for their return, their now thundering return,
rivers that pour from the sky.

OUT OF EARTH

Out of Earth, crystal essences
rise up, flowers distilled in radiant color
passed, as blossoms gift the bee to honey,
sweetness pouring out from purity refined
held shining, eyes before the sun,
color unimaginable and clear,
singing into day, echoing
from stars by night.

VIBRATION

Where are the bells of the old church,
the hours rung over the hill and field far,
a distant heart's recall to ourselves,
to turn away, on this revolving hour,
from the outward pull, to sink within that
bell's tone, following its call home,
to where we sound within, this richness
overflowing, so we are relieved,
our being filled as our emptiness made us,
solid crystal and pure gold,
ringing all the way through.

VIOLET

One violet light unfurled,
low upon the vine,
flows out intensity unmatched
by paint or lens or dye;
color all its own, angels gifted this one gift:
to be yourself, spiraled parasol of light;
for this one day blaze out
what others can but bow before—
beauty pouring out by being
only what you are.

IV

EACH STAR PLACED IN THE NIGHT SKY

Were there a way
    there is

to hold the unholdable,
    my arms and my hands surround you

to believe the unbelievable,
    I have always loved you

to bend to the Earth as a star,
    my caress, my breath, inflamed

and raise that light
    O bright enkindled heart!

to Heaven.

LIKE A RIVER, LIKE AN OCEAN

It's not one
you know, there
is no need of
stopping.
It goes on and on,
like breath,
like the evening sky;
the whole world flows out,
one word after another,
a song of no
beginning, where
day and night turn
like dancers.
We place these periods,
we hang a comma
like a hat,
but no one can find
anywhere
that anything
ends.

WE CAME TOGETHER

Wherever you fall,
we will be there
to catch you,

Under the water's swirl,
feel our strong arms,
our firm hand.

We tried to save ourselves,
and found instead
we were saving others.

We were not just light,
but stones and footholds,

We were hands pulling each other
from the drowning sea.

THE WAY THERE

It's a small room,
almost invisible.
You can only feel your way there,
like traveling the house at night,
using only your fingers;
there is birdsong, and
a soft breeze,
mostly a warmth
made of old loves and roses,
and a slanting evening sky.
Wandering in the day it's easy to miss—
most of the time you do.
It has a mirrored door,
that sounds cold I know,
but it's not, and as you reach for it—
there you are, arms opening wide
receiving yourself,
welcoming your
own smile.

DRAINING AWAY

The soft rain does
what soft rain does
so well,
washing away;
the draining down,
each drop
dissolves the one before,
replacing the moment
each moment,
the past,
takes it away,
all of it,
the grit and the
grief of each thought,
welling up to the rain,
the precious rain,
soft drop after
drop,
dropping,
oh with such grace,
washing away.

IT'S LIKE NOTHING

It's not like
liking, but love,
this letting everything go,
slipping into silence,
as into a warm bath in winter;
the way deliciousness
comes in, as everything else
goes out, as though when
all of it is gone,
something floats free,
and it is so light
and so clear
you never knew *anything*
this way before,
slipping out of self,
into silent soaring joy.

GIVING

And so the World came
in the warm afternoon,
reaching forward toward evening,
saying, *take me*,
and my taking was her giving,
completely,
what I had always wanted,
to fall completely in,
to be—so absolutely—
that all I desired was to empty,
to let it all pour out,
so that when the clear glass
was righted,
no one could find me,
and the only thing there was
was sunlight, shining upon her face,
her fields, her trees,
upon her beaming,
upon her glory.

LIKE WATER

It is like water taken up through the fingers,
the scent of mock orange and locust blossoms blown
from a summer day; it's the center of the stone,
within your own insideness, a cold flame wavering,
the white fluttering of a moth's wings.
It's your touch, touchless, pressing on the heart; it's
the way everything sits breathlessly, breathed by the light.
It's the window open in springtime, the lace curtains billowing out;
it's the pull like a push, as we roll over
the earth laughing, loving it all.

ONE STEP

Maybe it is as simple
as the blue sky,
the way the ripples run
from the stone,
the way the pebble sinks
straight down.
Maybe we walk right through,
one foot after another—
past the confusions
of form and color,
and then out,
into the light.

SAYING NOTHING

This wind-leaf speech, the bird chirp
chipmunk-chattering speech, this light-holed
bright flowerfield speech, this motion-dancing
limb reflecting high cloud traveling speech,
speaks without meaning, without reference,
without understanding, without construction;
only with being, touched upon the skin,
on the inside of eyelids, the tip of the nose,
the hair-lifted eyebrow, words right within
the heart, within the capillaried bone,
rising within the ear, saying nothing
we can understand, can do, can act upon,
can follow through, only for this instant,
only forever this fullness to be.

HOW IT IS

This is how it is:
everything, right now.

And after that,
everything, everywhere you look.

And then you leave,
you travel far way, and there it is:
everything, everywhere.

BODHISATTVA

The dark sky glows with watercolor lights,
the breeze blows down the hill and
through the trees, the humidity becomes bearable.
The rain is out there, over the horizon of the hazy trees,
making its long march from the midwest,
carrying lake and river water, gathered from
expiring fields and desiccated forests, who, having
so little and hastening their own end, say, *here,
take what I have, you want it anyway. Though I do not
understand, let it be a gift to another's life. Let my act,
through your unconsciousness, your power,
be for someone, a blessing.*

EVENING COMING ON

Beyond the pines the field is grey
after sunset. Birds scatter in the grass,
searching for insects cooled after the summer
sun. They run and stop. Their head dips,
they run again. Run, stop. Run, stop.

Behind the walnuts and oaks geese call, already
starting their southern run. A large crow soars overhead,
flapping his wings as he glides into the tall trees.

No leaves are moving anywhere.

It is almost too dark to write. A car drives down
the road, wobbling and flapping a flat tire:
flub-flub-flub-flub-flub.

I pull the black woven bookmark tightly
down the center of the page,
and close the book.

MORE THAN ENOUGH

Do you feel the space,
the presence between *things*,
the leap, the dive, the openness
that holds a billion worlds?
Can you feel the freedom flowing
between your out-stretched fingers, that lifts
the falling leaf, that winds between
the hairs upon your head?
There's room to live a thousand lives—
enjoying every one—between your
little finger and your slowly
waving thumb.

ONLY THE BUDDHA

Out of emptiness
the Buddhadharma gives you
someplace to return to:
working on an old koan,
studying the thousand sutras,
attempting to follow the precepts—
giving them *all* up,
after you've worked so hard, so long
with each of them—
who but the unseen, unknown Buddha
could cut the ropes and sink his raft,
walk shoeless and empty-handed
out upon that shore?

LOST IN MYSELF

Geese in the blue-grey sky—
lost in myself,
as the swimmer beneath the
blue-green waves;
all day, all night, weaving
my way through this
bright clear soul.

EVERYTHING WAS THERE

Everything was there when I woke,
what wasn't—the mind silent, the vast
field of contentment, the sky of satisfaction,
the single bark of a dog, the sweet sounds
overlaying the wind, the crickets in the fallen
leaves calling to the backhoes backing up,
then more dogs, a distant engine's roar
at the edge of my ear—it was a symphony
of world cacophony, harmonized,
caramelized, flowing like honey, made
beautiful by being what it wasn't, once
known as it was called, now known
as the music, the song, the symphony
of what it actually was.

UPON THE WALL

Upon my wall the light
that moves the leaves, the
shifting life that brilliance brings
within my soul, the sharp decline
of dark to light, the feathered fractal
dance of shadows weaving in
and out of form—and through the
window spirit blossoms into
orange and green and white, lit by
light into a brilliant blue—
moved by that great breath
that fills my chest, exhaling
adding in, the breath that fills
and moves the world, moves me,
moves you.

THE POSSIBILTY OF RULES

Silence can be measured in miles,
    Depth, by how far we see within
    when looking out,

Quiet, by sounds that rise and fall—
    a call that comes, and goes,
    and comes again.

Warmth, by that which spreads
    within the body outward,

Coolness, by love condensed and
    savored on the tongue—

Space, which we extend to fill
    by being,

Release, by letting go, by opening up,
    by letting everything that comes,
    come in.

UNHOLDABLE

Time flowed
into the cup, the bowl,
the body.
It was new time,
totally fresh,
clear and filled
with lights.
It was the joy of morning,
of life's promise,
of possibility;
it rose and flowed over,
down the sides,
into the cracks of
the past,
away,
unholdable—
still perfect, as new
as a robin's egg.
And the bowl filled
as it overflowed,
and it filled again,
with perfection;
and my hands were wet
with it,
and my face
refreshed,
as it came,
as it flowed over,
as it moved on.

WHEN IT IS

Is it in the next room?
Is it next week?
Is it when you're good enough?
Is it when you're older?
Is it when you fall in love?
Is it when your bills are paid?
Is it when you're happy?
Is it when you're sad?
Is it when you win the game?
Is it when you lose?
Is it when you're born
or is it when you die?
When exactly
is it?

V

OLD CROWS

The large black crow sails between
the trees, caws to his mates, his brothers
in their large black business, roustabouts chasing
smaller birds away, bullying in:
Our digs now you see, calling to their
friends—*It's party time*—loud and unruly, there goes
the neighborhood I guess—give us some
peace won't you!—but they've got a way
about them. Was it something I said? So
quiet now, the whole gang's taken wing,
and moved on down the road.

BETWEEN OUR FINGERTIPS

Oh bright book,
gathering in the news of the heart,
sung as only the moon could
sing to the sun,

your words, healing our thinking,
sending away doubt and dark imagining,
opening the road held between
our fingertips, offering

the joy of the way in.

THE SOLID WEIGHT OF BEING

Morning again.
I gaze from the shadow
of the trees into gold fields,
watching alfalfa wave in the sun.
Oak and maple edge the hill,
embracing sun and shadow.
All sinks in, settles, and
moves on through:
the solid weight of being.
And I am content, filled with gold,
with satisfaction, with everything
the world would never bring me,
and it is nothing—
yes, the fields, the sky, the sense of peace
in being are here too, yet when
I close my eyes we all are here,
rocking in the arms
of emptiness,
blessed in the breeze of bright well-being,
welcomed home
by everything that is,
by all the empty space
of every single thing.

KATHY

The day that Kathy died
the leaves were lit by their own light,
pale green below and bright gold above,
the sky was a bluer blue,
the air was a fresher air,
as though some precious gift
were opened, to escape,
to flow in the way
it always wanted, out
into the whole world.

—for Kathy Yoselson, (1946—2012)

BRILLIANCE TOO BRIGHT

Crows barking like dogs
like geese flying on the warm
autumn air flowing up from the
sunrise the brilliance too bright so
I block with my arm with my hand
while trying to write with the whole
out-of-doors pressing and pushing
at the edges of the glass of the window
trying succeeding to get in.

TURNING COLDER

The hurricane's wind has blown
down most of the leaves. Bare branches
stand against the mottled grey sky.
Clouds shift and turn colder, water feels
its sinking movement, its closeness to crystal.
Still the crows caw, motor cars drive
down unseen winding roads.
I make my morning coffee in the same
glass pot, and watch the woods for deer, a hawk,
a wandering fox. Wet leaves lie everywhere,
and I fall in love again with this day,
with all the strange bright beauty
of the earth.

IT IS TIME

Sometimes it takes a long time
for the quietness to come in,
an hour or a day, a week or a year.
The oaken door opens slowly,
and within the wine has sweetened,
old bottles of rich darkness,
their glint a deep red,
their savor their softness,
not their bite but their blessing,
which thanks you for waiting,
for abandoning the rush, the speed,
the accelerated whirling,
to give time to boulders,
to mountain walls,
to your own waiting for ripening,
that says now is the time,
now is what the waiting was for.

TASTED BY BEAUTY

Each taking away
leaves only wholeness,
that which leaves, reveals.
Even the core keeps
thinning, until there
is only air, complete seeing
through. Out of the invisible
the essential keeps arising:
new buds in the spring,
a stranger's sparkling eye.
Your inward breath
pulls every new thing into
being; your exhalation
lets everything go.
The night sky reveals
jewels beyond believing,
morning sun burns
all that imagining
into one blazing star.
Right now your heart longs
to dissolve into something
sweet like honey, to
be tasted by beauty, and
totally consumed.

A DIFFERENT KIND OF HOLY

It could all be here
if you let yourself listen
everything contained
in twenty lines of speaking
the complete exposition
of every proposition and
said with such grace
it would be one of those perfections
everything complete
with nothing left to flounder
a speaking of every thing
because the expression
is a wholeness
a different kind of holy
where truth forms the blessedness
for it speaks the way it is
not from resignation
not from a depression
but from a kind of glory
that a circle ends in roundness
and continues on forever
the way the music of these lips
says right now it is all
it is all for you

ENOUGH

This is the gift
of November morning sunlight
walking through the
quiet rooms
the house opening
before me
it will never be more
than this is now
every time
will be enough.

MORNING LIGHT

White morning light, incandescent
ice, flared upon the window wet,
frost reformed, crystal thrown through
cleanness, white and blinding
light, burning away light,
of what was left over: dirty clothes in
the corner, old papers and trash,
worn-out books, old loves and aggressions,
each catch fire, phosphorous burning,
ash like the air, almost not there,
caught by the wind, lifted away,
dropped over the earth, falling
to feed us, tilling it down,
growing into greenness, water to air,
air on the window pane, molecules
forming, fractured by freezing,
long fingers reaching, crystal receiving,
holding outflowing, white rays of intensity,
blindingly clear, white morning light.

THE SNOW

The snow and the heat
came at the same time,
the white ice and the green leaves,
the pink blossoms and the
kabuki mask, both
with a kiss, though the cold
froze, somehow it was
warmth I remember, a
taste of something like
a promise, like an almost
opened door to joy.

SATURDAY MORNING, 8:00 A.M.

They are back, like tiny
butterflies in springtime, the
first flakes of snow, for
this new year's winter, a few
here and there, almost countable,
then a flurry of wind and
the window is awash with them—
spinning up and down,
rushing one way or another,
to the tune of the low wind's roar;
now a whirl, now a vortex,
a snow tornado of tiny white dogs
chasing each other's tail.
The wind softens.
The roar returns.
And heavily, in familiar community,
by the thousands and thousands,
it really begins
to snow.

IN OUR BONES

We know in our bones
this will not last, none of it
ever did, all of it was its own
instant, the entire universe,
the stars, our small town, our house,
our family, the good times and
the bad, the joys and
the pains, each one molded
to the moment, unique among
all others, dissolving as we watched,
into something else, another particular
thing, a morning, a sunrise, and
we knew we were going somewhere,
by the way we could feel
the wind or the waves pulling,
then pushing from behind;
it all seemed the same, even as
it changed, as it slipped through
our fingers, as it shaped us to this shape,
these shoes, this taste, bringing
us moment by moment where
we always were, where we are now,
watching the wind blow,
reading these words…

WHEN I FELL INTO THE WORLD

When I fell into the world, it was
as into my mother's arms, it was into
the holding of warmth, the blue-green water,
it was into the beings who blinked
back at me amazed, as I was by them.
I fell from separateness, I fell from constriction.
I fell from the ice castle of myself, through
the rushing darkness, past screams,
past fear. I did not float up, I fell down,
and it was the world that waited
as I was stripped bare, as I tumbled out
of my self—faster and faster through blue
clouds and white, into the unknown arms
of joyfulness, toward the beings unnumbered
who opened their hearts in love.

ABOUT THE AUTHOR

Richard Wehrman has been a painter, jewelry designer, graphic designer, award-winning illustrator, and writer. He has been a student of Zen Buddhism, the School of Spiritual Psychology, and the Diamond Approach. He lives with his wife in Upstate New York. This is his third book of poetry.

*

This collection gathers poems written between 2010 to 2012.